SEED TO BONE

SEED TO BONE
POEMS

MARIAN WILLMOTT

VERMILION BOOKS

ISBN: 979-8-218-63341-7

Cover painting by Marian Willmott
www.willmott studios.com

VERMILION BOOKS

Contents

For Anika, Indigo and Lucas

TIME MOVES

Fifty-five Years Together

Each morning before rising
he reaches for my hand
his eyes seeking mine.

A kind of drowning.
A kind of waiting.
A rescue.

Each day we walk in the wind
sculpting a ritual of pleasure,

carrying each other forward
into the twilight
near the edge of existence.

Who are we
without a god—

body like a seed,
blood like a river,
belief like a stone.

Each night we dine
in the glow of candle light—
a reminder of the sweetness

in what's been lost,
in our time together now
and the time we have left.

Childhood Secret

Not far into the woods
outside of time
under low hanging branches
a hidden room
pine-scented floor
walls of woven shadow
crickets and crows
a rock that was my friend

No one knew
I lived alone like this

Black Leather

Long hair hid one eye.
I did not know what I wanted
only what they did.

I knew the difference between
a hard edge and a dull one—
which would cut the other
and how the armor of a face
masks what is given up.
I knew the power of a black leather jacket
and a bottle of gin under the bed,
how the siren of my body held
a ticket to somewhere else.

It was years before I knew
the way flesh could soften,
the way my breasts
would swell and ripen
with the sweetness of milk.

A Quiet Untangling

Before you swerved and rolled the car
you wore your family like a hat—
proper but slightly cocked,

a burgundy veil spiced with a feather,
your long hair twisted into a bun.
The knot of your apron

securely tied, you let your hands
dance above the floured dough
the way a bird flies to the nest

to feed its young.
You hated to weed
but arranged cut flowers

with the same tenderness
you tucked me in at night,
knowing how they wilt and fall.

But I watched each stitch
of your hand-made clothing
with growing impatience.

At sixteen, I left clutching the back
of a stoned boyfriend,
his motorcycle spitting gravel,

my long hair flying.
You stood in the kitchen doorway
like a painting framed by begonias,

the diamond on your arthritic finger
shining like a beacon in a storm.
I returned, my back bruised

from a barn's rough-hewn floor,
my hair ratted and snarled.
Everything that mattered

left unsaid, you set to work
pulling, parting, combing,
a quiet untangling.

Plate with a Blue Rim

The male bird-of-paradise
fans and pulsates its feathers,
struts sideways and cocks its head.

You wear button fly Levi's,
never a zipper, a shirt
tucked in, Italian shoes.

I used to like the feel of my body
pressed against your back,
arms clinging to your torso,
the motorcycle seat between our legs,
the necessity to lean with you around a curve
as you flirted with danger and speed.

Sometimes your fist
became hard as a hammer,
lines drawn.
There were nights
the door was left ajar
and betrayal slipped in—
knives glinted in their drawer.

All that is history,
it's been over fifty years.
You tie on an apron, roast vegetables
and make a marinade for scallops,
serving my dinner
on the one plate with a blue rim.

You take me firmly
by the wrist and lie me down,

touching me intently, waiting, watching
playing me, a long crescendo,
like I am an exotic instrument
and you are enraptured by my song.

Dark Matter

we call undetectable matter "dark matter"
for it is the light not the matter that is missing

Three days have been spent on this painting,
reworking value and hue,
changing color harmonies.
    color exists only in wave lengths of electromagnetic energy

Three days ago the emergency room called.
These are hard cold facts—
there was a bar, my son--a stranger,
edgy words, rugby team,
he was drunk, they were drunk.
    emotions travel on neural circuits
    connect limbic system, neocortex

In half sleep I startle
to scenes of tearing flesh,
clenched jaws, steel-toed
boots, blood's thick stain.
I number from memory
the bones in my son's face,
my rigid muscles unable to curl
into dream again. He called me,
X-rayed skull, nose reset, philosophical.
    dark matter appears to dwarf luminous matter
    by a factor of at least 10, possibly as much as 100

I keep trying shades of gray,
searching for the weight of clouds,
the river's turbulence, the way leaves
scatter pieces of day on the forest floor.

the existence of brightness and color belonging
to the object itself is purely psychological

I want to capture the shadow's
fall and rise in descending darkness,
the glow darkness holds onto
after the sun disappears.

Still Life, Requiem and an Egg

I've heard it said, a day
is like an egg, full of possibility—
but cracked, scrambled or hard boiled,
it makes a difference.

At a local church this afternoon
a choir sang Mozart's Requiem,
chords, heavy and full reverberated
in the vaulted ceiling,
the soprano's high notes, unearthly.

A large crucifix hung on the wall,
sculpted in detail with drips of red paint.
I tried to imagine a nail
hammered through my hand,
or harder yet, the ice grip
of the one wielding the hammer.

Tonight the wind howls
and pelts the glass with sleet.
I'm curled under a quilt
sewn by my daughter
from my dead mother's clothing.

In the morning I'll cook a blue egg
slid from under a warm, feathered belly,
boil it three minutes and scoop it—
smooth and slippery—
into a porcelain cup.

I've started a still life painting—
two bowls and an urn.

I'll spend the day
as though all that matters
is how light creates form,
how shadows deepen interiors
and how color can sing—
prayerful chords in a minor key.

Near the Tomatoes

My son left home this morning
heading for the coast

leaving behind a box of books,
taking any pots and pans

I had to spare.
At the market I catch myself

in the mirror above the dead fish,
gray-haired and frowning

wearing his bad-ass T-shirt.
Across the aisle a neighbor waves,

long black dress hanging
from her bent frame.

We ask after each other,
Death, she says,

I'm nearing death.
We're near the tomatoes,

shiny and smooth. I cup
their taut skin, surprise

my bony fingers
with seeds and sticky juice.

Mother and Daughter

It's been three years
since I've seen you,
a chasm voice cannot bridge.

I miss what the hand can hold,
what touch creates,
how eyes do more than see.

Did I tell you I had breast cancer?
Worry sifts the soil of time.
My face an apparition in the mirror

traced with lines, a relic of memory.
Last night my long dead mother
called out to me.

Tread lightly. I see you
watching from the moon
riding the unicorn of the young.

My pasture of snow
holds the prints of the wolf,
moon-lit rivers of ice.

I can only offer
the north star to guide you
until we hold each other again,

our hands shining like river rocks,
ashes of fear swirling downstream,
the ocean on our tongues.

Evening

I sit in a room no longer familiar.
Rain washes the walls gray,

a slight breeze splinters light across
pictures of a bride and groom.
My tongue rests soundless

on a songs last note.
It rains for hours.

I wrap myself in a moth-eaten blanket,
fold napkins, sort socks.
Someone is walking on water

giving away free question marks,
dragging the bottom for dreams.

A young girl draws in mud,
stones for eyes, ferns for hair,
a deep hole for the mouth filled

with rainwater, small bones, leaves
and broken glass. She stirs and stirs.

I find a few words I've never spoken,
words saved for a lover or a prayer
and dry them off for her.

She sings to herself, outlining
walls for a house, a kitchen, a bedroom.

I close my eyes and listen—
night falling.

Blue Ice

Deep winter.
I look for signs of life
in pristine snow—

tracks of deer, rabbits,
or the coyote's hunt.

Last night I opened
a letter my grandfather wrote
to be read if he didn't return
from France in WW1,

his heart filled with love and duty
and the promise of a peaceful world.

That night I dreamt of a woman
holding a severed head
in her arms, as if carrying
the world's broken promises.

There is always blame,
enemies to hate,
Bible pages set on fire.

Cracks in the frozen pond
form an undecipherable score—
patterns etched by wind and stars—

silent music of the soul,
life's longing
written in blue ice.

Cannot

A blue mountain oversees
the valley, trees green and swaying.
If it had words it would say,
all is as it should be.

But there are lands,
claimed and named
in languages foreign to my ear,
valleys rife with artillery fire.

News from near and far converge,
no longer divisible.

I cannot fathom the sight,
of bodies—calloused hands
and pony tails—shot down,
scattered in a field,

a field perhaps blooming
with buttercups, clover, and daisies
like the ones I just picked.

I'll brush the petals from the table
as they fall with the same gratitude
I closed my father's eyes,
his features at rest,
the ache of love blossoming.

Can heartbreak be weighed?
The weight of one bullet
tips the scales.

The River Rushes

The river rushes by
with a force, a persistence,
    undulating patterns of
    earth brown and sky silver.

From the air
the river branches out
    veins in earth,
    like veins of trees, of bodies.

A teenager balances
on the bridge railing,
    taunting white water and rock
    twenty feet below.

My grandmother, distraught,
left her house in winter,
waded into river's frigid water
    until it flowed over her,
    unwavering.

The river rushes by
with a force, a persistence.
I write to listen,
to feel its power in my bones,
    to feel
    what I cannot know.

Time Moves

Time moves like a large animal
heaving its body to stand.

The past is a silver trout circling under ice,
at night it becomes the moon.

Sun follows shadows of birds.
Broken mirrors glitter in landfills,

dust erases the future.
Each morning we wipe the window clean.

We make pictures out of stars,
replace loved ones with a headstone.

A distant voice calls you awake,
calls your scarred name,

a voice like a gong
in an empty cathedral.

Words turn into the howls of wolves,
tongues harden into bone.

We follow five steps to the present moment,
to the last breath of the one beside you.

Eyes opened or closed,
feet frozen or a finger in flame,

heart in a vise or in song,
the last page cannot be read.

HOLD DEEP

Wind Sweeps In

Wind sweeps in,
herding black clouds,

lightning's snaking tongue
lashes out,
thunder beats the glass.

Peaches, flowers, and jars of honey
tremble on the window sill,
the dog hides under the bed.

Clouds shift and hustle,
time removes its mask,
rivers open in the sky.

Shafts of light
like revelations,
break through,

a sliver of something more,
something else,
something unnamable.

I step outside…

Hold Deep

Not a word.
A thick fog hangs
over the deserted beach.

Dead minnows
abandoned by tide's surge
stink in tangles of seaweed.

I carry with me
the cold stone of loss,
the silence of sorrow.

Each step
molds wet sand, leaving
a constellation of my passing.

I put the perfect spiral
of a snail shell in my pocket,
a gull dips and soars.

The horizon disappears,
no beginning or end,
my skin is salt spray and wind.

Thoughts and worries,
dissolve, giving way
to surf's rhythmic insistence.

My driftwood bones
hold deep
the wings of this day.

Veins of Rivers

Bridges are precarious
if you walk on the railings—
the river has no saints.
You might not know the other side,
the way thorns grow sideways,
their small piercings.
You pretend you don't see
the way lovers say goodbye.
I only want to be reassured,
to know my veins
are the veins of rivers,
flowing from head to mouth,
swirling like fingertips
stroking the bones of the dead.
If you shut your eyes
and listen with ears like fish
you can travel downstream.
We don't need a map.
We'll let the current take us.

Beneath

The sound of nothing,
of moth wings.

What we remember of the dead.

Our former selves dreaming within,
another day simmering beneath today.

Hours turn, seed to bone.

Language—a boat, our hands—oars,
the unknown swirls below.

Candle Moon

Night arrives with its candle moon,
romancing the dead and past lifetimes,

scary stories and childhood monsters
warned by the owl from a dark forest.

Souls of sinners and soldiers move
in silence, knives rusted and dulled,

sadness marked by small stones,
white as first frost. Stars sing

in deep pools where dreams hide,
forgotten and remembered—

flying weightless over fields,
a virgin with child,

the dead calling our names,
a stallion running wild—

the drumming hooves,
our beating hearts.

Each morning I rise
to find day already begun,

my body gone and reformed,
my name a cloud

slowly condensing,
the secrets of the night,

whispering
in the hands of day.

Threads

I'm talking to myself again.
Words cripple this pencil
trembling in my hand—
never enough, never right.

Take the carnation—
too red and showy
or the lipstick smile—
teeth, too white, denying
their bite, rip and tear.
I like the tongue's
lick-cluck-whistle.

I'm holding threads
of unraveled years—
over half my life forgotten.
I've lined up small bones
on the windowsill.
A spider's web reaches
the skull I picked out of the sand
when wind blew my hair into wings
and the horizon was on fire.

I remember returning home
to a fresh cherry pie
centered perfectly
on a white tablecloth,
a small red stain,
a hunger,
and the taste of salt
wild on my lips.

Wail

A saxophone wail
sweeps across the barroom.

Mirrors catch faces
with animal eyes,

jewels at the throat
flame with desire,

revealing an understory—
bones of broken vows,

debris of grief,
orgasm's undertow,

ashes of dream.
Bodies begin to move

with the thrust of bass,
idle chatter falls

like forgotten pennies,
jailed minds open,

armor dissolves
in the glow

of surrender,
the spice of it all.

Love Letter

Seagull scream,
white-winged fall
into blue's open mouth
where it all converges
or breaks apart.
We hunt for fish scales tangled
in seaweed beds, our tongues
write love letters while regret
wanders among wild grasses.
We ease across the beach in skin capes,
our names turned to shells,
low tide's wet sand
giving away each footprint
as we lose each other
again and again.

Candle-lit words roll
on the tongue, fine
little grains harboring lemon,
worlds beyond ours.
We climb easily into quarter notes,
one over the other,
long fingers feeling their way
under black and white,
sliding to the hand held open.
Each night, just before day
a fox hunts in the meadow
with the grace of your arm
circling my waist, your lips
moving across my throat.
My mouth holds still the O
of an owl, watching

from a lightening scarred tree.
What is there left to hold onto?

Who can give X a value,
multiply what is unsaid?
Underneath a silver sheen
fish shadows flicker,
too numerous to number.
Notice the heat of the hand
as it moves along the thigh,
then subtract the stone of silence,
the space between cool blue
and warm yellow, distances
opening and closing,
a bluefish gasping in air.

Your gaze follows me;
I have lifted the hair from my neck.
Still air grows heavy with rain,
the water's surface placid, reflective,
waits for our freckled bodies
to break through, surrender
to our hearts' deep dive.

Black Feather

Dawn.
Endless expanse of ocean,
silver sky, an empty beach—
nothing more.
A Chinese painting, the Tao.
Identity meaningless—
woman, wife, white.
Everything changing, timeless.

An American flag at the top of a dune
catches my eye, waving, insistent,
as if someone wearing red and blue stripes,
a bandolier sash of bullets and diamonds,
was strutting down the dune towards me,
commanding I listen.

(In my poem, they wade into the ocean,
re-appear barefoot, clothing bleached white,
hardware gone, silent as a fish.)

The sun rises higher,
silver slides into cerulean,
brightly colored umbrellas will soon dot the beach.
I find a black feather and leave it
upright in the sand, a small prayer
quivering in the morning light.

Acorn

I'm nestled in the shade
on the edge of a salt marsh
where a blue heron fishes.
Distant dunes blaze
pink in early light.

An acorn just dropped
by my foot—
it's all the company I want.

I hear a door shut,
someone yells.
I try to curb
mind's ticking warnings—
Did a car just pull up?
Is the door locked?
Is anything wrong?
Did I leave the stove on?

The heron glides to another spot
leaving ripples of light,
the blue of the distant bay
intensifies as the dunes
turn to gold.

Another acorn drops.

Rock

I am walking away
from the world,

from my mind flashing
news headlines, untold disasters.

Only the cawing crow
cares where I am.

The path ahead disappears
in fern's quivering geometry.

I stop to rest on a rock
abandoned by history,

veins of moss.
I'm at home

in rock's timeless company—
an ancient piece of star,

part of our galaxy's 400 billion.
I close my eyes, quiet

my brain's 86 billion neurons,
a silence, almost—

a whir of energy—
star, stone, body,

humming,
becoming one song.

Beacon

Walking with my sadness
in trees quiet immensity,
lost in the wanderings

of my mind,
my name unravels,

my blind feet
follow the braille
of roots and stones

into the prayer
of shade's cathedral.

A crack of underbrush
alerts my animal self—
a deer's flag flashes white—

a beacon from the wild,
a halleluiah in the day.

March

Snow weeps,
its bridal white stained brown,
decay and grit of old loves.

You can be lonely anywhere,
tired of who you are.
Ice melts one slow drip at a time,

snakes stir underground,
a promise of apple blossoms.
It's time to strip down,

expose the pale skin
of your scarred breast,
shed the bloodied coat

of your dark battlefield
and hold the icicle like a sword
against the heat of your tongue.

Far from the River

I walk the perimeter
of what I cannot know,

       like a dog circling
       before lying down.

Dreams brew within
like incantations,

       every loss numbered
       like an old psalm.

I fear the world's
love of battle,
its leaps into fire,

       far from the river, far
       from walking on water.

I have no answers.
Death will douse the flames
of belief and opinion.

       Out of grief's ashes,
       beyond world's dark web,

you can hear
the angels singing.

IN A MINOR KEY

This Is Not the End

River rain mist
I cannot sleep
a turbulence of desire,
a spiraling of days,
dreams of peaches
open and juicy.
I'm erasing straight lines
and formulas to live by.
Never mind gravity,
what about black holes?
Rocks block the way,
but this is not the end.
This is the way
rivers meander.

Planting

*A Sacred Fig, the Sri Maha Bodhi, is over 2,000
years old, the oldest known flowering plant*

In the midst of battle—
blood tests, biopsies, CT scans—
I collect sayings:

Every cloud has a silver lining,
Live in the moment,
Belief is half of healing.

I write each on a scrap of paper
ball it up and till it into damp soil.

Can you hear the frogs?
All day and into the evening they sing.

Scientists chart orbits, measure light.
Life expectancy is a scientific mean.
Even ocean's jagged shoreline
can be seen as a fractal pattern.

I like to watch stars fall,
feel the urgency
of moon's pull in my blood.
I want to drink the heat of sun's fire.

A soft rain approaches,
clouds thicken.
I'm down on my knees,
digging with my hands,

cultivating tomorrow—
seed   compost   mulch.

Skin

Skin: (1) Snakes shed it in the woodpile
     (2) A mummy's is more brittle than ancient
        parchment
     (3) If cut with the jagged edge of a mirror
        below the cheekbone it confines you to a
        psyche ward
     (4) It stabilizes the body's temperature

You can only sense the blood
coursing underneath—
you can't peel back
the layers and dive in.
Touch the surface—
the pores, moles, the occasional hard
scars that hint at ancient entrances—
the belly-button that spirals
inward, scars of childhood mosquito
bites scratched to scabs and picked,
small bloodlettings.

Beyond the surface
(sweaty, powdered, tan, light, dark, freckled,
wrinkled, smooth, sagging, lifted, dry, oily, oiled,
shaved, plucked, stitched, tattooed, pierced, bruised)
feel
the swell of belly, the cut
and reconstructed right breast
the sharp bone
that rages underneath.
Move your hand slowly.

breast's lament

I was
desire's pyramid
mother's milk
night sugar
how in love
with me you were
gift
to your lover
nipple kissing pink
tongue and jewel
hands held cupped
warmed my skin until
losing
me to knife's
steel sliced hard
passion sunken
nipple skewed
cloth closed hidden
your lover
dreams his hands
hold me
scar blazing
but you wear
regret's
black stone
around your neck

Ouroboros

Behind closed lids
there is solace
in silver light,
my stitched together flesh,
soothed and delivered
into dream
as night clouds
darken the moon
and wild eyes glow red.
I steal seeds from the wind
and plant them
in my barren womb,
feet wading into river's open mouth.
I carry two gifts,
one in each boney hand.
The left holds a snake
swallowing its tail,
the right, flowers -
yellow, purple and pink -
petals, softer than skin.
Sleep, falls like rain.

Ouroboros: an ancient symbol of a snake swallowing its tail
found in many cultures, usually related to the cyclic nature
of the universe.

Trip to Italy

I wander out on paved goat paths,
 without language, without markers.
A coliseum holds the heat
of day's sun, seats
smooth and rounded
from the ebb and flow of people,
a stone vessel, steady
through the turmoil of years.

In a Venetian palace, gold filigree
surrounds paintings that cover
the ceilings and walls with Biblical scenes
in a palette of urgent darks,
commanding lights, soft full breasts
in an orgy
of longing and tragedy.

On the street
tourists press against each other,
a man catches a pickpocket snatching
his gold watch, Italian mini cars zip
by women in mini-skirts,
breasts swelling over tight black tops.

I wear loosely draped clothing,
the scar on my right breast
jagged and red—
a fresco cracked in mid-story,
a fault in time's boundary line.

I retreat to the dark silence
of a church to rest my swollen feet,
strangely at home in the presence
of towering stone arches,
ancient tombs.

If the Moon Comes Out

If the moon comes out
I'll skinny dip,
lower my imperfect body
into black river fire,
scars glinting like fishbones
where a breast used to be.
Clouds cross the sky
like apparitions.
There are no sharks,
only undercurrents of fear.
When did I stop diving
for shiny stones?
I will float on moon ripples,
grassy banks alive with fireflies.

Counter Top

I arrive just after a thunder storm,
my sister's down
30 pounds to under 98.

She's faced with the insurmountable
task of carrying a tea bag
from cup to garbage,

the counter piled high
with week old dishes, plastic
containers, jars, bottles,

waiting to be washed.
I brought a painting
to hang over the table—

an orange circle glowing
through transparent blue,
a metaphor, say…

the light within.
But here in her dark falling
I put on rubber gloves

and begin to scrub:
sponge, dish soap,
scouring pad, and now

the counter top—
yellow and shining.

The Coming Night

We can't see the river from here—
the bank drops sharply,
a deep cut
to rock, snaking
through forest's interior.

We sit on the grass,
the day a small gift.
Your body is down to bone,
it's flesh translucent.
We count the number of times
we each read The Black Stallion,
reliving an old love,
your dying
surfacing in the pause
between words.

Leaves hang motionless,
afternoon shadows spread
across the grass like coats
flung down, bodiless forms,
the coming night
quieting the day.
We listen—
the sounds of the river, endless.

The Company I Keep

I walk into the mouth of the woods,
moving in a fog of thought until

a vision pierces its veil—
blue pieces of a robin's egg

fluorescent on the dark dirt
and its fresh yellow stain.

I don't ask why.
A wild turkey struts

fretfully into the underbrush—
I too, am another animal.

A rotting tree stands erect,
barren limbs out spread.

Stage 1 or 4? No matter—
a feasting place for woodpeckers,

a sanctuary for squirrels.
Here, I watch things come and go.

Where Waves Break

Hairless, bony and ashen,
my sister's head
lies on a white pillow,
looking like the skull
it is becoming.

I rush to her,
she responds with a plea,
don't remove the oxygen mask—
her link to life,
whether the first breath or last.

I take her hand, already cool.
We were a mirror for each other.

Now I hold her ashes—
gritty, not fine like wood ash—
wade in where waves break
and watch them swirl,
then disappear.

I find some peace here
where we last walked together.

I listen to the ocean's
steady rhythm,
heartbeat of the body
that holds her now.

In Velvet

Thick with red eyes glowing,
night descends into the house,
100,000 billion galaxies expanding

and spiraling above.
Alone, will fear always seep
into the soles of my feet?

Sometimes an unfinished crossword
left in a chair, a sweater
draped over the arm

reminds me of your absence.
I've been taking walks,
hunting for small treasures,

enticed by mystery—
the geometry of a beehive,
the way water carves into stone,

how unearthed bones
piece together histories.
How many have a tooth saved,

wrapped in velvet, buried
in the back of a drawer?
I keep the hand-like bones

of a flipper found in the sand.
The bones of our hands
are particularly complicated,

especially the fingers—
what we cannot hold
and what we can.

What Remains

In night's frozen quiet,
moonlight exposes backs
of whale mountains, quivers
tree shadows across the snow
like Chinese brush strokes.
I have treasures that speak
the night. When my children
left home, I found a mouse skeleton
hidden under a tiny pair of socks
in the back of my son's closet.
I said goodbye to the socks—
I saved the bones: delicate
skull and ribs, curled legs,
tail arched stiffly into space,
time's calligraphy. After
my mother's death, I found
three strands of silver hair
clinging to her dark blue
housecoat hanging in her closet.
Her long hair was wild and loose
in the morning before
twisting into a bun. Now
her hairs remained,
alive and dancing.

Entrance or Exit

Roots twist through damp
decay and mushroom villages,
part artery, part bone.
Arched branches
narrow the forest path—
an entrance or exit.

Light dims to shadow,
a snake flashes its magic.
There are other worlds,
dreams that haunt.

I remember my mother's hand,
gnarled like bark,
lying on a white sheet.

Last night I dreamt I found
a family of turtles in my pocket.

Ordinary stones wet with dew
glow with silver light,
lichen glitters gold
on a fallen tree—
pleasure resurrects
a broken body.

I like the dampness,
how it softens the ground,
seeps slowly into my shoes,
cousin to my tears.

My mother stroked my forehead,
smoothing back my hair,
her body scent enveloping me,
the way leaves,
rustling underfoot,
perfume the forest.

Sometimes I Go to the Cemetery

Heavy, permanent, imposing,
wide as a headboard,
the polished granite guards
their bones,
lying below, side by side.

I lie down,
opening my heart
to feel a presence
but only a tall pine's quivering shadow,
brittle needles and reptile roots
embrace me.
They are not here.

My father is in his leather chair
lighting his pipe.
My mother is doing a crossword puzzle,
legs tucked under her.

Or she is rising,
dripping from the bath
while I watch with fascination
as she dries herself,
patting lilac powder
into her belly's fleshy folds,
under each heavy breast,
between her thick thighs,
her body ripe, soft and sweet smelling.

The stone
only marks their time

blind
to the tendrils of their arms
entwining and blossoming.

Murmurs

Sleet stings the night window,
wind courses through trees,

the electricity blinks off,
the house, a small vessel

abandoned at sea,
creaking and moaning.

A candle carves
 a small circle of light

in ghost shadows,
dark rooms echo

murmurs of past goodbyes,
of being forgotten.

     ***

In the morning
sun burns through frost,

rooms fill with light,
shadows retreat.

Empty spaces
begin to hum

like my mother used to hum
cutting vegetables, stirring soup.

Turning

Animals wait in shadow.
Morning's soft yellow

turns to noon's piercing heat.
The calendar on the wall

marks the day with a square
as though beginnings

and endings
could be contained.

I fear you're leaving me—
slowly, tornados

of dust in your bones.
Your flesh will turn blue,

you'll call to me
from the bottom

of an evening lit field—
white winter words.

Night will hold out its empty cup,
moon will fill it with silence.

Red Boat

Maybe it's the Catholic in me
she laments, trying to make sense.
Her mother is refusing treatment,
preparing for her death.

A bright red bird with a black wing
lands in a tree near us, blazing
like the dingy in the harbor
swinging slowly on its mooring
in late afternoon light,
turning from fiery red to bone black
and back to fire again.

I could take her hand,
climb into the dingy
and row toward the horizon,
watch the sun sink,
clouds glowing
like embers in an ashen sky,
as her suffering mother
flies free—
red bird with a black wing.

Fish-Woman

Last week, at two o'clock,
a memorial service,
the week before, three o'clock.

Today I've gone to the lake,
wind-rippled water shimmering
into the hazy hues
of the Adirondack Mountains.

I swim away from shore
as far as I dare, a dark dot
in blue's immensity
and dive towards the bottom,
below light filtering down,
seaweed hair streaming,
breast stroke and frog kick
into the womb
of a silent underworld,

until I have to breathe again,
bursting back into the dazzle of day,
gasping, skin tingling, reborn,

as if I'd been on a long journey
and met a wizened old fish-woman
who laughed and took my hand.

As My Friend Lies Dying

Death has stained my reality,
ink dark spreading.

In a bookstore,
amidst a turmoil of voices,

I find solitude
in the blank page of my notebook.

I thought I could
relinquish life gracefully,

but sidewalk smiles elude me now,
sweetness becoming too bitter.

I tried to buy something, a bit
of happiness but couldn't decide.

The clerk explained death
brings beauty and art—

words recited
like lines in a play.

I prefer the coyotes' howls,
their crying yips, breaking

the silence of night—
what haunts, half real, half remembered.

I begin to write,
letting words pause and dip

through layers of thought,
edging my way below sadness,

submerged beyond any definition of self—
until moonlit words

begin to brighten
beneath the veil of darkness.

ECHO OF MYSELF

Where the Road Ends

My skin registers the change—
the road dead ends, woods take over,
my house disappears.

Here the coyote caches its steal,
trees tower over my silenced voice,
leaves whisper my thoughts.
A river cuts its way through
rock ledge and splintered bone,
exposed tree roots grip the bank,
snaking into earth's heart.

All day and night, water licks
the rocks, its white foam
becoming small wings in moonlight.
Memories sink like stones
in the river bed, the current
swirls over them
leaving an echo of myself.

If I were a winged fish
I would dance in leaf shadows.
I collect odd-shaped stones,
name the things
I don't want to let go of,
the people I never want to leave.

Pink

Pink has
 a sweetness, a deceit,
a fantasy, ranked by beginner angels.
I don't wear pink.

I'm in love with the silent expanse
of white snow fields,
their blue shadows
sculpting bone-like forms
uncluttered by life's green
tangle of growth and decay.

Every muscle in my body aches
from gravity's ride, each birthday
a rock-climb with hooks and ropes
gazing at the rapture
of free fall, untethered.

Dear young woman, why
are you wearing pink stiletto heels?
Leggy, sexy, easily toppled.

Sex is one glass of wine
and a garlic-stuffed olive,
its urgent pull and dangerous undertow
have eased to a gentle ebb,
soothing violin's bitter-sweet
tears of broken vows.

I listen, hair faded to gray, to white
but my tongue sings out,
pink, moist and sensate,

defying me, refusing
every melancholy note,
like a wild salmon
leaping upstream,
as it must.

The Weight of a Name

The sun sinks,
taking with it

the noise of the world.
The moon rises

huge and blood orange,
spilling its reflection

across a breathing black sea.
A first star appears, jewel

above dune's soft-curved silhouette.
My cells will someday join the spectacle.

I draw my initials in sand,
carving deeply

the weight of a name—
its scales of self-worth,

its armored shell—
and wait for my marks

to be licked and merged
with ocean's salty tongue.

Ocean Resurrection

Wind swirls salt and surf
into the air rising
like a musical crescendo

calling forth wings,
calling for surrender,
to be stripped free

of theory and belief,
of all that doesn't matter—
to walk on the edge of being

River Mirror

I've been watching myself,
the river a mirror.
    My face has nothing to do with it.
    My eyes are black stones.
    Rain breaks the surface
    into silver spirals.
Give me this day, nothing holy.
The reflection of the old woman
    is not mine,
    only the jewel of memory
    hanging from her neck.
    I didn't want my fortune told,
    I never had a plan.
I could be a tree
arcing over the river
reaching toward the light.

Fading

I sip morning tea
and begin my ritual puzzle.

I treasure my pen,
its soft grip and easy flow.

Today the marks
look like ghosts,

fading more
with every stroke.

I hate to toss it—
I've held it

so many mornings,
each one a seed of peace.

I know—
it is just a pen.

Everything fades—my hair,
brown to grey, now white

shining silver in the sun—
like an aura,

or the flash
of an angel's wing.

The Empty Dog Collar

I weeded the garden this morning
but it could have been a dream—
the veil between reality and dream
thinning, tangled in memory's underbrush.

As a teenager I read *The Illusion of Reality*
and walked city streets wearing a button,
"I am your perception of me",
dragging an empty dog collar
clinking on the sidewalk behind me.

Everything a question,
everything unknowable.

Now Google's algorithm for me
produces a lucid dreaming course—
a way to ease into death
using *The Tibetan Book of the Dead*.

I'll return to the garden,
the green of life throbbing,
interwoven melodies
of decay and bloom
singing to my aging body—
a timeless dream.

The Body

A moving object, separate like a tree or river
that ripens, withers, bleeds, pulses.

A collection of organs, pathways, connections,
a geometry of cells, the illusion of solidity.

A vessel, an antenna collecting the touch of breeze
before thunder, silver light on green leaves.

A flaw, fretted over, an imperfect rendering,
masked, polished, presented.

A hunger, an animal hunger.

A seeded garden, a pear blossom,
ocean swell just before cresting.

A mummy's brittle parchment,
a prayer of bones,

A dematerializing, fire to ash,
weighing less than the ashes
of one campfire, tossed
to the wind.

My body will be easy

My body will be easy.
What of my paintings,

their continuous search
to unveil the light.

My journals—
the ones I cannot bear to read again,

crumbs to the witch's house,
its darkness, its oven, its struggle.

Light a fire,

save a few pieces of my heart—
its deep woods and moonlit sea—

for my children and grandchildren
on their journeys,

to hold
in their darkness.

High Tide

Last night we sat on the ocean beach until dark,
lulled by the hugeness of it all,
our bodies still vital enough to seek one another,
lives entwined, almost inseparable,
our time waning.

Tomorrow we will return to the home
that holds our past like a skin—
a clay horse our daughter made,
a spot on the ceiling
where our kids threw spaghetti,
a wooden spoon with a carved handle
I've held for over half a century.

I've been excising—scalpel and forceps,
drawings the mice got into,
years of old Christmas cards,
a palomino pony bleeding its stuffing,
love of my childhood.

Morning sun ignites the dunes
as we return to the beach.
High tide has erased our footprints,
the place we sat last night holding hands.

We walk in silence
letting icy waves break
over our bare feet
and sand warm them again.

Heart

Heart: Body's engine—arteries, valves, and pump
      Fueled by breath
      Rivers of veins
      Cupid's target
      Tribal drummer

A tattoo, a Hallmark card, an emoji
(romance, caring, sympathy, friendship,
bleeding or broken,
blood red or rainbow colored)

Too often our hearts harden,
cling to dogma, create enemies
then pray the angels will sing
when the heart stops.

We fear the last beat, DNA patterns pixelating,
dissolving, dispersing into the universe—
black holes, expansion and contraction,
spirals, gases and flames, stars,
planets, earth, a flowing river,
a tree, this day,
this moment,
this love.

Storm of Days

The grace of movement slows,
body's posture sinks
towards stone.

Mind soars at sunrise,
then dips,
tied to flesh and bone.

We grapple
with the laundry of thought,
its stains of fear and loss,
the torn fabric of what matters.

As the storm of days
quiets
and wind dies,
we fall into ourselves,

cast off
the anchor of our bones,
let our names
float downstream,

and raise
the sail of our hearts
to carry us
towards evening's first star.

About the Author

Marian Willmott is a writer and visual artist, enjoying both the solitude of the Vermont mountains and a vital artistic community. She received a BA in painting and psychology and an MFA in painting. Writing and art have both been an integral part of her life since childhood. She raised a family and taught art part time in the public schools, always finding time to walk in the woods and focus on her own creative work. She strives to stay present to the mystery we are a part of and deepen the encounter.

Acknowledgements

Thank you to the following literary journals who published my poetry:

As Above So Below: "Acorn"

American Writers Review: "Hold Deep"

Barely South Review: "Fish Woman"

Birmingham Arts Journal: "High Tide"

Black Fox Literary Magazine: "Sometimes I Go to the Cemetery"

Blood & Bourbon: "Threads," "Murmurs," "The Weight of a Name"

Blueline Literary Magazine: "If the Moon Comes Out"

Calyx: "Counter Top"

Comstock Review: "What Remains"

Denver Quarterly: "Where the Road Ends", "Skin" (2004)

Karamu: "Dark Matter"

Rough Diamond: "breast's lament," "Skin" (2025)

Salamander: "Turnings"

The Louisville Review: "Pink"

The Worchester Review: "In Velvet"

Thank you to the following Anthologies for including my poetry:

Gilbert and Hall Press: *Alchemy and Miracles Anthology*
Pioneer Valley Breast Cancer Network: *Unbearable Uncertainty*

Thank you to the following presses who published my two poetry chapbooks:

Pudding House Press, *Turnings*
Prolific Press, *Still Life, Requiem and an Egg*

A huge thank you for the invaluable support of my poetry group and family.

www.ingramcontent.com/pod-product-compliance
Lightning Source LLC
Chambersburg PA
CBHW051329120626
46547CB00016B/2463